A REPORT TO CONGRESS
IN ACCORDANCE WITH § 356(c)

OF THE

UNITING AND STRENGTHENING AMERICA BY PROVIDING APPROPRIATE
TOOLS REQUIRED TO INTERCEPT AND OBSTRUCT TERRORISM ACT OF 2001
(USA PATRIOT ACT)

SUBMITTED BY

THE SECRETARY OF THE TREASURY,
THE BOARD OF GOVERNORS OF THE FEDERAL RESERVE SYSTEM,
THE SECURITIES AND EXCHANGE COMMISSION

The staff of the Commodity Futures Trading Commission also assisted in the preparation
of this Report.

December 31, 2002

A REPORT TO CONGRESS
IN ACCORDANCE WITH § 356(c) OF THE USA PATRIOT ACT

TABLE OF CONTENTS

I.	Introduction..1	
II.	Background..2	
	A. Evolution of the Bank Secrecy Act as a Tool to Combat Money Laundering and Terrorist Financing 2	
	B. The Crimes of Money Laundering and Terrorist Financing........................5	
	1. Codification as Federal Crimes...5	
	2. Stages of the Money Laundering Process...7	
	3. Use of Investment Companies in Money Laundering.......................7	
III.	Effective Regulations to Apply the BSA to Investment Companies.....................10	
	A. Registered Investment Companies...11	
	1. Mutual Funds...12	
	2. Closed-End Funds...15	
	3. Unit Investment Trusts..17	
	B. Unregistered Investment Companies..19	
	1. Hedge Funds..19	
	2. Commodity Pools..24	
	3. Private Equity and Venture Capital Funds.....................................26	
	4. Real Estate Investment Trusts ("REITs")......................................29	
	5. Proposed Rule for the Application of the BSA to Unregistered Investment Companies..31	
IV.	Personal Holding Companies..35	
V.	Recommendations...36	

I. Introduction

On October 26, 2001, the President signed into law the Uniting and Strengthening America by Providing Appropriate Tools Required to Intercept and Obstruct Terrorism Act (USA PATRIOT Act) of 2001, Pub. L. No. 107-56 ("USA Patriot Act"). Section 356(c) of the USA Patriot Act calls for a report to Congress ("Report") within one year from the date of enactment containing recommendations for effective regulations to apply the record keeping and reporting requirements of the Bank Secrecy Act, Titles I and II of Pub.L. 91-508, (the "BSA") to investment companies and personal holding companies.[1]

---

[1] Section 356(c) of the USA Patriot Act provides:

Section 356 – Reporting of Suspicious Activities by Securities Brokers and Dealers; Investment Company Study

* * *

(c) REPORT ON INVESTMENT COMPANIES.–
    (1) IN GENERAL. – Not later than 1 year after the date of enactment of this Act, the Secretary, the Board of Governors of the Federal Reserve System, and the Securities and Exchange Commission shall jointly submit a report to the Congress on recommendations for effective regulations to apply the requirements of subchapter II of chapter 53 of title 31, United States Code, to investment companies pursuant to section 5312(a)(2)(I) of title 31, United States Code.
    (2) DEFINITION. – For purposes of this subsection, the term "investment company" –
        (A) has the same meaning as in section 3 of the Investment Company Act of 1940 (15 U.S.C. 80a-3); and
        (B) includes any person that, but for the exceptions provided for in paragraph (1) or (7) of section 3(c) of the Investment Company Act of 1940 (15 U.S.C. 80a-3(c)), would be an investment company.
    (3) ADDITIONAL RECOMMENDATIONS. – The report required by paragraph (1) may make different recommendations for different types of entities covered by this subsection.
    (4) BENEFICIAL OWNERSHIP OF PERSONAL HOLDING COMPANIES. – The report described in paragraph (1) shall also include recommendations as to whether the Secretary should promulgate regulations to treat any corporation or business or other grantor trust whose assets are predominantly securities, bank certificates of deposit, or other securities or investment instruments (other than such as relate to operating subsidiaries of such corporation or trust) and that has 5 or fewer common shareholders or holders of beneficial or other equity interest, as a financial institution within the meaning of that phrase in section 5312(a)(2)(I) and whether to require such corporations or trusts to disclose their beneficial owners when opening accounts or initiating funds transfers at any domestic financial institution.

In accordance with section 356(c) of the USA Patriot Act, the Secretary of the Treasury (the "Treasury"), the Board of Governors of the Federal Reserve System (the "Federal Reserve Board"), and the Securities and Exchange Commission (the "SEC") submit this Report. The staff of the Financial Crimes Enforcement Network ("FinCEN") and the Commodity Futures Trading Commission (the "CFTC") also assisted in the preparation of this Report. Specifically, we address three questions raised by section 356(c) of the USA Patriot Act: (1) what are the appropriate "effective regulations" to apply the requirements of the BSA to investment companies; (2) which of those regulations should be applied to investment companies to best achieve the goals of the BSA; and (3) what investment companies should be subject to the BSA regulatory scheme?

II. Background

A. Evolution of the Bank Secrecy Act as a Tool to Combat Money Laundering and Terrorist Financing

Congress passed the BSA in 1970 to prevent the use of cash payrolls for tax evasion and to provide tools to fight organized crime. Until last year, the stated purpose of the BSA was "to require certain reports or records where they have a high degree of usefulness in criminal, tax, or regulatory investigations or proceedings."[2] The original focus of the BSA was on banks, which are the main financial institutions that deal in cash.

As the nature and sophistication of financial institutions have grown, new and creative ways to hide sources of illegally obtained profits have been devised. To protect the U.S. financial system from criminal activity and to promote the detection and prosecution of financial crimes, Congress added anti-money laundering provisions to the BSA in 1992, which authorized

---

[2] 31 U.S.C. 5311. Language expanding the scope of the BSA to intelligence or counter-intelligence activities to protect against international terrorism was added by section 358 of the USA Patriot Act.

Treasury to apply the law to many different types of financial institutions.[3] Prior to the passage of the USA Patriot Act, regulations applying the anti-money laundering provisions of the BSA were issued only for banks and certain other institutions that offer bank-like services or that regularly deal in cash. These regulations require such financial institutions to take the following actions:

- Keep records related to certain monetary instrument purchases and funds transfers;[4]

- Report currency transactions of more than $10,000 by, through, or to the financial institution;[5]

- Report the transport of currency across U.S. borders;[6]

- Report certain accounts that United States citizens and residents hold at foreign financial institutions;[7] and

- Report suspicious transactions relevant to possible violations of the law.[8]

Title III of the USA Patriot Act amends the BSA to make it easier to prevent, detect, and prosecute international money laundering and the financing of terrorism by:

- Requiring that every financial institution establish an anti-money laundering program that includes, at a minimum, (i) the development of internal policies, procedures, and controls; (ii) the designation of a compliance officer; (iii) an ongoing employee training program; and (iv) an independent audit function to test the program;[9]

---

[3] 31 U.S.C. 5312(a)(2). Treasury also has broad authority to adopt rules requiring other types of businesses to adopt anti-money laundering programs if those businesses deal in cash (31 U.S.C. 5312(a)(2)(Z)) or engage in activities that Treasury determines to be "similar to, related to, or a substitute for" activities engaged in by one of the listed businesses. 31 U.S.C. 5312(a)(2)(Y).

[4] *See* 31 CFR 103.29, 103.33.

[5] *See* 31 CFR 103.22.

[6] *See* 31 CFR 103.23.

[7] *See* 31 CFR 103.24 and 103.25.

[8] *See* 31 CFR 103.18, 103.19, 103.20, and 103.21.

[9] *See* section 352 of the USA Patriot Act.

- Requiring Treasury to prescribe, jointly with the federal functional regulators, regulations setting forth minimum standards regarding the verification of the identity of any person seeking to open an account;[10]

- Requiring each U.S. financial institution that establishes, maintains, administers, or manages a private banking account or correspondent account in the United States for a non-U.S. person to take certain anti-money laundering measures with respect to such accounts;[11]

- Prohibiting certain financial institutions from establishing, maintaining, administering, or managing a correspondent account in the U.S. for a foreign shell bank (other than certain foreign shell banks with regulated affiliates);[12] and

- Permitting financial institutions, their regulatory authorities, and law enforcement authorities to share information regarding persons engaged or reasonably suspected, based on credible evidence, of engaging in terrorist acts or money laundering activities.[13]

The USA Patriot Act required the extension of the anti-money laundering requirements to financial institutions, such as investment companies, that had not previously been subjected to BSA regulations.[14] The USA Patriot Act also added new entities to the statutory definition of financial institution, such as futures commission merchants, commodity trading advisors ("CTAs"), and commodity pool operators ("CPOs").[15]

In accordance with the USA Patriot Act, FinCEN, in conjunction with other federal financial regulators, has adopted or has proposed for adoption rules to implement the amendments to the BSA. These rules prescribe anti-money laundering program requirements for certain financial institutions[16] and require certain financial institutions to implement reasonable

---

[10] *See* section 326 of the USA Patriot Act.

[11] *See* section 312 of the USA Patriot Act.

[12] *See* section 313 of the USA Patriot Act.

[13] *See* section 314 of the USA Patriot Act.

[14] *See* section 352 of the USA Patriot Act.

[15] *See* section 321 of the USA Patriot Act.

[16] *See, e.g.,* Anti-Money Laundering Programs for Financial Institutions, 67 FR 21110 (April 29, 2002); Anti-Money Laundering Programs for Money Services Businesses, 67 FR 21114 (April 29, 2002); Anti-Money Laundering Programs for Mutual Funds, 67 FR 21117 (April 29, 2002);

procedures to verify the identity of persons seeking to open accounts.[17] The regulations also prohibit certain financial institutions from establishing, maintaining, administering, or managing a correspondent account in the U.S. for a foreign shell bank (other than certain foreign shell banks with regulated affiliates)[18] and require certain financial institutions to implement due diligence programs for certain correspondent as well as private banking accounts.[19] In addition, FinCEN promulgated a rule that sets forth procedures for information sharing between federal law enforcement agencies and financial institutions and voluntary information sharing among financial institutions.[20]

B. The Crimes of Money Laundering and Terrorist Financing

1. Codification as Federal Crimes

In 1984, Congress passed the Money Laundering Control Act ("MLCA"), which made money laundering a federal crime.[21] The financing of terrorist activities or of designated foreign

---

Anti-Money Laundering Programs for Operators of a Credit Card System, 67 FR 21121 (April 29, 2002); Anti-Money Laundering Programs for Unregistered Investment Companies, 67 FR 60617 (September 26, 2002); Anti-Money Laundering Programs for Insurance Companies, 67 FR 60625 (September 26, 2002).

[17] *See* Customer Identification Programs for Banks, Savings Associations, and Credit Unions, 67 FR 48290 (July 23, 2002); Customer Identification Programs for Certain Banks (Credit Unions, Private Banks and Trust Companies) That Do Not Have a Federal Functional Regulator, 67 FR 48299 (July 23, 2002); Customer Identification Programs for Broker-Dealers, 67 FR 48306 (July 23, 2002); Customer Identification Programs for Mutual Funds, 67 FR 48318 (July 23, 2002); Customer Identification Programs for Futures Commission Merchants and Introducing Brokers, 67 FR 48328 (July 23, 2002).

[18] *See* Anti-Money Laundering Requirements -- Correspondent Accounts for Foreign Shell Banks: Recordkeeping and Termination of Correspondent Accounts for Foreign Banks, 67 FR 60562 (September 26, 2002).

[19] *See* Anti-Money Laundering Programs; Special Due Diligence Programs for Certain Foreign Accounts, 67 FR 48348 (July 23, 2002).

[20] *See* Special Information Sharing Procedures to Deter Money Laundering & Terrorist Activity, 67 FR 60579 (September 26, 2002).

[21] 18 U.S.C. 1956 and 1957.

terrorist organizations is also a federal crime.[22] These crimes, like the vast majority of federal white-collar crimes and offenses traditionally associated with organized crime, also serve as predicate acts for the crime of money laundering.

One section of the MLCA criminalized the conduct of a "financial transaction" involving proceeds that are known to derive from some "specified unlawful activity."[23] A transaction is a "financial transaction" under the statute if it involves monetary instruments, the movement of funds, the transfer of title to property, or the use of a financial institution.[24] To be guilty of money laundering under this section of the MLCA, the defendant must act with the intent to (1) promote the carrying on of a specified unlawful activity, (2) engage in tax fraud, (3) conceal or disguise the nature, location, source, ownership or control of the property, or (4) avoid a transaction reporting requirement.[25] Thus, this section criminalized "smurfing" – the practice of intentionally structuring transactions to avoid reporting requirements by splitting the total amount of funds available for deposit into amounts below the $10,000 reporting threshold.

Another section of the MLCA criminalized the engagement in a "monetary transaction" involving property of a value greater than $10,000 that is known to derive from a criminal offense, and that is actually derived from a "specified unlawful activity."[26] The term monetary transaction is defined broadly to cover almost any transaction by, through, or to a financial institution, including the deposit, withdrawal, transfer, or exchange of funds or a monetary instrument.[27] Unlike the section of the MLCA discussed in the paragraph above, this section

---

[22] 18 U.S.C. 2339A and 2339B.
[23] 18 U.S.C. 1956.
[24] 18 U.S.C. 1956(c)(4).
[25] 18 U.S.C. 1956(a)(1).
[26] 18 U.S.C. 1957.
[27] 18 U.S.C. 1957(f)(1).

does not require the defendant to know that the property was derived from a specified unlawful activity. Rather, this section requires the defendant to know only that the property was derived from some criminal offense. Therefore, a defendant cannot rely on willful blindness to avoid liability under this section of the MLCA.

2. Stages of the Money Laundering Process

The process of money laundering is accomplished in three stages. The first stage in the process is placement. The placement stage involves the physical movement of currency or other funds derived from illegal activities to a place or into a form that is less suspicious to law enforcement authorities and more convenient to the criminal. The proceeds are introduced into traditional or nontraditional financial institutions or into the retail economy. The second stage is layering. The layering stage involves the separation of proceeds from their illegal source by using multiple complex financial transactions (*e.g.*, wire transfers, monetary instruments) to obscure the audit trail and hide the proceeds. The third stage in the money laundering process is integration. During the integration stage, illegal proceeds are converted into apparently legitimate business earnings through normal financial or commercial operations.

3. Use of Investment Companies in Money Laundering

For purposes of the Report, an investment company is defined broadly to include those entities listed in the definition of the term in the 1940 Act, entities that would be investment companies under the 1940 Act but for the exceptions provided in certain sections of the 1940 Act, and certain other pooled investment vehicles that are not subject to the 1940 Act because they do not invest primarily in securities. The money laundering risks associated with investment companies generally are discussed below.

a. Placement Stage

Investment companies can be used by criminals at every stage of the money laundering process. Investment companies are less likely than other types of financial institutions (*e.g.*, banks) to be used during the placement stage because they rarely receive from or disburse to investors significant amounts of currency. However, money launderers appear to have used investment companies at this initial stage. FinCEN has received a number of reports concerning the use of a stolen, altered check to establish an account with an investment company. Other suspicious activity observed in the purchase of investment company interests includes the use of money orders and travelers checks in structured amounts to avoid currency reporting by the financial institution issuing such instruments. Similarly, money launderers have purchased an initial interest in an investment company with several wire transfers, each in an amount under $10,000 and from different banks and brokerage firms.

b. Layering Stage

Money launderers are most likely to use investment companies in the layering stage of the money laundering process. Money launderers can use investment company accounts to layer their assets by sending and receiving money and rapidly wiring it through several accounts and multiple institutions, or by redeeming an interest in a company originally purchased with illegal proceeds and then reinvesting the proceeds received in another investment company. In fact, a number of reports have described the use of wire transfers, checks, cash, and money orders to deposit money into an investment company account, followed by withdrawals from the account on the same day or during the same week.[28]

---

[28] *Cf. Correspondent Services Corp. v. J.V.W. Investments Ltd.,* 120 F. Supp. 2d 401 (S.D.N.Y. 2000) (noting that account was frozen by financial services firm due to concerns with possible money laundering involving purchases of mutual funds and other investments).

Layering may also entail the purchase of an interest in an investment company in the name of a fictitious corporation or an entity designed to conceal the true owner. Beyond that, criminals themselves may even create investment companies to conceal further the source and ownership of illicit proceeds. For example, the facts of a case decided by the Court of Appeals for the Eleventh Circuit in 2001 demonstrate how drug smugglers created an elaborate money laundering operation utilizing three different investment companies to launder funds.[29] The defendants in this case converted cash obtained from drug sales into cashier's checks. They then deposited the cashier's checks in a shell company located in Liechtenstein. Through a web of other sham investment companies, the defendants were able to move the funds to the United States and "loan" it back to themselves. The deposit of the cashier's checks in Liechtenstein prevented authorities from tracing the drug proceeds to their final destination. Similarly, any attempt to trace the source of the loan in the United States would reveal only that the loan was from a foreign entity protected by bank secrecy laws.

c. Integration Stage

Finally, investment companies may be used in the last stage of the money laundering process: the integration of illicit income into legitimate assets. For example, if an individual redeems an interest in an investment company that was purchased with illegal proceeds and directs the investment company to wire the cash from the redemption to a bank account in the individual's own name, the wire transfer would appear legitimate to the receiving bank. Moreover, money launderers sometimes organize a sham investment company to defraud investors or clients and to make payments from the company's account to their personal accounts appear legitimate. For example, in one case a defendant organized a venture capital firm to

---

[29] *U.S. v. Gilbert*, 244 F.3d 888, 893-897 (11th Cir. 2001).

defraud clients seeking capital for business ventures.[30] He used the venture capital firm to operate an advance-fee scheme by which he would agree to obtain funding for a client within a certain time frame in exchange for a sizable up-front fee. Never intending to fund the business projects or return the advance fees, the defendant deposited the money in the firm's account and then proceeded to write large checks on the account made out to third parties and himself.[31]

III. Effective Regulations to Apply the BSA to Investment Companies

Different types of investment companies have different susceptibilities to money laundering, requiring variations in the regulatory approaches to them. To be effective, regulations applying the requirements of the BSA to investment companies must reflect the particular investment company's structure and vulnerability to being used in one or more stages of the money laundering process. In this section of the Report, we provide a description of the types of investment companies that currently exist, any special vulnerabilities that a certain type of investment company may have to being used for money laundering or terrorist financing, and the action taken or recommended to apply the provisions of the BSA to these companies.

The first step in drafting the regulations that would apply the requirements of the BSA to investment companies is to define the term "investment companies." A broad definition of "investment company" could include a large range of entities from small investment clubs to large corporate holding companies and, in between, an array of financing vehicles many of which are unlikely to be used for money laundering purposes. The discussion below reviews the various types of investment companies within two categories—those registered with the SEC under the 1940 Act and all others.

---

[30] *U.S. v. Davis*, 226 F.3d 346, 348-349 (5th Cir. 2000).

[31] *See also U.S. v. Mullens*, 65 F.3d 1560 (11th Cir. 1995) (using an investment company to operate a Ponzi scheme).

A. Registered Investment Companies

Section 356(c)(2) of the USA Patriot Act indicated that the definition of "investment company" provided in the 1940 Act should be the starting point in crafting an appropriate definition. The 1940 Act defines "investment company" to include any issuer of securities that is, or holds itself out as being, engaged primarily in the business of investing, reinvesting, or trading in securities.[32] Most investment companies offered to the public are registered with the SEC under the 1940 Act, which subjects them to a comprehensive scheme of regulation.

The 1940 Act classifies almost all registered investment companies as either "management companies" or "unit investment trusts."[33] Management companies, which often adjust (or "manage") their portfolios in an active manner, are subclassified as "open-end" and

---

[32] Section 3(a)(1) of the 1940 Act defines "investment company" as any issuer that (A) is or holds itself out as being engaged primarily, or proposes to engage primarily, in the business of investing, reinvesting or trading in securities; (B) is engaged or proposes to engage in the business of issuing face-amount certificates of the installment type, or has been engaged in such business and has any such certificate outstanding; or (C) is engaged or proposes to engage in the business of investing, reinvesting, owning, holding, or trading in securities, and owns or proposes to acquire investment securities having a value exceeding 40 per centum of the value of such issuer's total assets (exclusive of Government securities and cash items) on an unconsolidated basis. 15 U.S.C. 80a-3(a)(1).

[33] A "management company" is any investment company other than a unit investment trust or a face-amount certificate company. 15 U.S.C. 80a-4(3). A "unit investment trust" is an "investment company which (A) is organized under a trust indenture, contract of custodianship or agency, or similar instrument, (B) does not have a board of directors, and (C) issues only redeemable securities, each of which represents an undivided interest in a unit of specified securities, but does not include a voting trust." 15 U.S.C. 80a-4(2). A "face-amount certificate company" is "an investment company which is engaged or proposes to engage in the business of issuing face-amount certificates of the installment type, or which has been engaged in such business and has any such certificate outstanding." 15 U.S.C. 80a-4(1). A "face amount certificate" is "any certificate, investment contract, or other security which represents an obligation on the part of its issuer to pay a stated or determinable sum or sums at a fixed or determinable date or dates more than twenty-four months after the date or issuance, in consideration of the payment of periodic installments or a stated or determinable amount" or "any security which represents a similar obligation on the part of a face-amount certificate company, the consideration for which is the payment of a single lump sum." 15 U.S.C. 80a-2(a)(15).

"closed-end" companies. An open-end investment company is a management company that is offering or has outstanding any redeemable securities that it issued.[34] Open-end investment companies, which are more commonly called "mutual funds," are by far the most prevalent type of registered investment company and may be the most susceptible to being used for money laundering.[35]

1. Mutual Funds

Mutual funds are today one of the most popular ways individual investors participate in the securities markets. In 2001, more than 8,300 active mutual funds, with approximately $7 trillion in assets, were registered with the SEC.[36] Mutual funds are held by more than half of U.S. households.[37] A mutual fund, like any other investment company, is a trust, partnership, or corporation whose assets consist of a portfolio of securities, interests in which are represented by the shares that the fund issues. A mutual fund raises money from shareholders and invests it in accordance with the fund's stated objectives. Mutual funds are generally grouped into stock

---

[34] 15 U.S.C. 80a-5(a)(1).

[35] The staff of the SEC estimates, based on filings with the SEC, that as of December 2001, approximately $6.97 trillion was invested in U.S. mutual funds (including $741 billion invested in open-end management companies that fund variable life insurance and variable annuity contracts, and $23 billion invested in open-end management companies that are exchange-traded funds), $130 billion was invested in closed-end funds, and $121 billion was invested in unit investment trusts other than insurance company separate accounts (including $59.5 billion invested in unit investment trusts that are exchange-traded funds). As to investment companies that fund variable life insurance and variable annuity contracts, *see infra* pp. 20-21. As to investment companies that are exchange-traded funds, *see infra* note 50.

[36] Investment Company Institute, Mutual Fund Fact Book (2002) ("ICI Fact Book") 7. The SEC staff estimates that as of December 2001, there were approximately 3000 registered investment companies that were open-end management companies. The staff further estimates that 1400 of these investment companies are "series companies" with an aggregate 7200 portfolios. A "series company" is a registered investment company that issues two or more classes or series of preferred or special stock, each of which is preferred over all other classes or series with respect to assets specifically allocated to that class or series. 17 CFR 270.18f-2. The assets allocated to such a class or series are commonly known as a "portfolio." The series or portfolios of a series company operate, for many purposes, as separate investment companies.

[37] *See* ICI Fact Book, *supra* note 36, at 24.

funds, bond funds, and money market funds.[38] In addition, like most investment companies, mutual funds usually do not have their own employees. One or more third-party service providers (which may or may not be affiliated with the mutual fund) conduct all of a mutual fund's operations.[39]

Unlike other investment companies, a mutual fund typically offers its shares continuously to the public, and redeems its shares on demand by investors, at a price based on the fund's net asset value.[40] A mutual fund usually offers its shares to the public through a principal underwriter, which is a registered broker-dealer.[41] Shares also may be purchased directly from some funds (called "direct-sold funds"). In addition, they may be purchased through a variety of alternative distribution channels, such as fund "supermarkets" (through which investors may purchase shares of several different mutual funds), insurance agents, financial planners, and banks.[42] Mutual funds employ transfer agents to conduct recordkeeping and related functions.[43]

---

[38] Mutual funds also may specialize their investment objectives in certain ways, such as by geographic location, industry sector, or the type of security in which they invest.

[39] A mutual fund may be organized or sponsored by an entity such as an investment adviser that provides other financial services. Thus, a mutual fund's investment adviser may simultaneously provide investment advice to individual clients, act as the investment adviser for other registered investment companies, and provide investment advice to unregistered pooled investment vehicles such as hedge funds. Mutual funds may also be part of larger complexes of entities that provide financial services. Other entities in the complex (*e.g.*, broker-dealers and investment advisers) will, of course, have employees.

[40] Mutual funds issue "redeemable securities," which entitle the holder to receive, upon presentation to the fund, the holder's approximate proportionate share of the issuer's current net assets, or the cash such share represents. 15 U.S.C. 80a-2(a)(32).

[41] On April 22, 2002, the SEC approved NASD Regulation Rule 3011 and New York Stock Exchange rule 445, which require their member broker-dealers to develop, and a member of the firm's senior management to approve, programs designed to achieve and monitor compliance with the BSA and related regulations. *See* Order Approving Proposed Rule Changes Relating to Anti-Money Laundering Compliance Programs, Securities Exchange Act Release No. 45798 (April 22, 2002) [67 FR 20854 (April 26, 2002)].

[42] Generally, insurance agents, financial planners, and banks that sell mutual fund shares must also be registered as broker-dealers. The alternative distribution channels for mutual funds usually maintain omnibus accounts with the mutual fund whose shares they distribute. In such case,

Because mutual funds typically offer and redeem their shares continuously, money launderers may invest in mutual funds due to the ability to obtain access to their money. To ensure that mutual funds take adequate precautions against such risks, FinCEN issued an interim final rule on April 29, 2002 that requires mutual funds to develop and implement an anti-money laundering program ("AML") reasonably designed to prevent them from being used to launder money or finance terrorist activities.[44] In addition, FinCEN and the SEC jointly published in July 2002 a notice of proposed rulemaking that would require mutual funds to establish customer identification programs ("CIPs").[45]

These rules, in mandating mutual funds' BSA obligations, recognize the particular way in which mutual funds are organized. They permit mutual funds to delegate responsibilities for implementation of an anti-money laundering program to one or more service providers or

---

neither the fund nor its transfer agent typically knows the identities of the individual investors. *See* note 43 *infra,* discussing the duties of transfer agents.

[43] Transfer agents maintain records of shareholder accounts, calculate and disburse dividends, and prepare and mail shareholder account statements, federal income tax information, and other shareholder notices. Some transfer agents prepare and mail statements confirming shareholder transactions and account balances, and maintain customer service departments to respond to shareholder inquiries.

[44] *See* 67 FR 21117, *supra* note 16. The program must meet four minimum standards. First, it must establish and implement policies, procedures, and internal controls reasonably designed to prevent the mutual fund from being used to launder money or finance terrorist activities, including, but not limited to, achieving compliance with the applicable provisions of the BSA and the implementing regulations thereunder. Second, the mutual fund must provide for independent testing by fund personnel or by a qualified outside party of its program to ensure compliance with the applicable portions of the BSA and implementing regulations. Third, the mutual fund must designate a person or persons responsible for implementing and monitoring the operations and internal controls of the program. Fourth, the fund must provide ongoing training to appropriate persons regarding the BSA requirements relevant to their functions and the recognition of possible signs of money laundering that could arise in the course of their duties.

[45] *See* 67 FR 48318, *supra* note 17. The proposed regulation would require mutual funds to implement reasonable procedures to (1) verify the identity of any person seeking to open an account, to the extent reasonable and practicable, (2) maintain records of the information used to verify the person's identity, and (3) determine whether the person appears on any lists of known or suspected terrorists or terrorist organizations provided to investment companies by any government agency. The comment period for the proposed rule ended on September 6, 2002.

intermediaries. These intermediaries, through which investors purchase interests in mutual funds, include broker-dealers and banks, which are required to have their own anti-money laundering and customer identification programs.[46]

2. Closed-End Funds

A closed-end investment company (or "closed-end fund") is a management company other than an open-end investment company.[47] Like a mutual fund, a closed-end fund is a trust, partnership, or corporation whose assets consist of a portfolio of securities, interests in which are represented by the shares that the fund issues.[48] Closed-end funds differ from mutual funds in that they do not offer their shares continuously, nor do they redeem their shares on demand.[49] Instead, a closed-end fund issues a fixed number of shares, which typically trade on a stock exchange or in the over-the-counter market.[50] Investors seeking to buy or sell these shares must

---

[46] Virtually all intermediaries that can hold mutual fund shares in an omnibus account are or may be subject to various anti-money laundering or SAR requirements. For example, a broker-dealer or investment adviser can hold shares for customers in omnibus accounts. Broker-dealers are already covered by the BSA's anti-money laundering provisions (including SAR reporting), and Treasury may extend these provisions to investment advisers.

[47] 15 U.S.C. 80a-5(a)(2). The staff of the SEC estimates, based on filings with the SEC, that as of December 2001 there were 632 registered closed-end funds, with aggregate assets of approximately $130 billion. The majority of these funds are publicly traded. The SEC staff estimates that as of December 2001 there were 54 closed-end funds, with assets of approximately $11.4 billion, that were not publicly traded. These funds are registered with the SEC solely under the 1940 Act.

[48] Recently some closed-end funds have registered with the SEC that invest predominantly in securities issued by hedge funds. *See* Robert H. Rosenblum & Leigh M.P. Freund, *A Primer on Structuring Registered Funds of Hedge Funds*, 9 Inv. Law 4 (Apr. 2002). As to hedge funds generally, *see* section III.B.1. *infra*.

[49] Section 23(c) of the 1940 Act [15 U.S.C. 80a-23(c)] generally prohibits a registered closed-end investment company from purchasing any security of which it is the issuer except on a securities exchange, pursuant to a tender, or under such other circumstances as the SEC may permit by rules, regulations, or orders designed to ensure that the purchases are made in a manner or on a basis which does not unfairly discriminate against any holders of the securities to be purchased. *See infra* notes 54 - 57 and accompanying text.

[50] Other types of registered investment companies may also be traded on a stock exchange. These "exchange-traded funds" or "ETFs" are registered with the SEC as open-end funds or unit investment trusts ("UITs"). Unlike typical open-end funds or UITs, ETFs do not sell or redeem

buy or sell them through a broker-dealer on the exchange. Like other publicly traded securities (and unlike the shares of a typical mutual fund), shares of a closed-end fund trade at a market price that fluctuates and is determined by supply and demand in the marketplace.[51]

Closed-end funds typically do not have an account relationship with their investors. As a result, those funds (and their service providers) are not in a position to detect and prevent money laundering. Purchases and sales of closed-end fund shares are effected through broker-dealers or banks, and these entities are already subject to anti-money laundering regulation.[52] For these reasons, closed-end funds do not appear to present a risk of money laundering that would be effectively addressed by subjecting them to additional regulation, and Treasury has not extended BSA regulatory requirements to closed-end funds.[53]

Although most closed-end funds do not redeem their shares, a category of closed-end funds – "interval funds" – do have limited redemption features. Interval funds rely on rule 23c-3

---

their individual shares at net asset value. Instead, ETFs sell and redeem ETF shares at net asset value only in large blocks (*e.g.,* 50,000 ETF shares). National securities exchanges list ETF shares for trading, which allows investors to purchase and sell individual ETF shares at market prices throughout the day. ETFs therefore possess characteristics of traditional open-end funds and UITs, which issue redeemable shares, and of closed-end funds, which generally issue shares that trade at negotiated prices on national securities exchanges and are not redeemable. The SEC staff estimates, based on filings with the SEC, that as of December 2001, there were nine separately registered investment companies, four UITs and five open-end funds, offering such securities. The SEC staff further estimates that as of December 2001, the five open-end funds offered 98 series with aggregate assets of approximately $23 billion, and the UITs had aggregate assets of approximately $59.5 billion. The separate series of a registered investment company that is a series company operate, for many purposes, as separate investment companies. *See supra* note 36 (discussing registered investment companies that are series companies).

[51] The price of closed-end fund shares may be above or below the fund's net asset value per share. This price differential is commonly referred to as a premium or discount, and reflects the market's assessment of the value and liquidity of the fund's portfolio assets, among other things.

[52] *See* 67 FR 21110, *supra* note 16.

[53] In April 2002, Treasury temporarily exempted investment companies other than mutual funds from the requirement that they establish anti-money laundering ("AML") programs. *Id.* Treasury stated its intention to continue to consider the type of AML program that would be appropriate for these companies, including the extent to which they pose a money laundering risk that is not more

under the 1940 Act to periodically offer to repurchase from shareholders a limited number of fund shares at net asset value.[54] Rule 23c-3 describes the intervals at which such repurchase offers may be made (three, six or twelve months)[55] and the amount of stock that may be the subject of a repurchase offer (not less than five percent nor more than twenty-five percent of the fund's outstanding stock).[56] There are currently an estimated 30 interval funds.[57]

Because investors in an interval fund control neither the timing nor the amount of the issuer's repurchase offer, the redemption features of interval funds do not appear to present significant money laundering risks. Accordingly, Treasury has not extended BSA regulatory requirements to interval funds, but it may reconsider this issue if the SEC were to liberalize the circumstances in which interval funds may make repurchase offers.

3. Unit Investment Trusts

A unit investment trust ("UIT") is a registered investment company that buys and holds a generally fixed, unmanaged[58] portfolio of securities and then sells redeemable shares (called "units") in the trust to investors. UIT investors receive a proportionate share of dividends or interest paid by the investments.[59]

---

effectively covered by the AML program of another financial institution through which investors purchase and sell their interests (*e.g.*, a broker-dealer or insurance company). *Id.* at 21117-21118.

[54] 17 CFR 270.23c-3.

[55] 17 CFR 270.23c-3(a)(1).

[56] 17 CFR 270.23c-3(a)(3).

[57] This estimate is based on filings with the SEC on Form N-23C-3 [17 CFR 274.221] during 2001.

[58] A UIT has no investment adviser and no board of directors.

[59] The 1940 Act defines a "unit investment trust" as an investment company that (i) is organized under a trust indenture, contract or similar instrument, (ii) does not have a board of directors, and (iii) issues only redeemable securities that represent undivided interests in a unit of specified securities. *See* note 33 *supra.* As discussed above, in April 2002, FinCEN temporarily exempted investment companies other than mutual funds from the requirement that they establish AML programs. *See* 67 FR 21110, *supra* note 16. Therefore, UITs currently are not subject to BSA regulatory requirements.

There are two types of UITs. The "traditional" UIT is sponsored by a broker-dealer, which deposits securities into a trust and offers interests ("units") in the trust to brokerage customers. Although these units can be redeemed, sponsors typically support a secondary market into which redeeming shareholders sell. These traditional UITs have many of the same characteristics of mutual funds that can make them attractive to persons seeking to launder money. However, they are entirely creatures of their sponsoring brokerage firms, which are already required by the BSA to establish AML programs and report suspicious transactions in connection with such entities.[60] It does not appear that applying anti-money laundering rules to this type of UIT would appreciably decrease the UIT's risk of being used for money laundering, and thus such application has not been made.

The second type of UIT is an insurance company separate account.[61] These separate accounts issue variable annuity contracts and variable life insurance policies, and invest the premiums received by the insurance company in one or more mutual funds. In this arrangement, the UIT separate account functions as a conduit to the underlying mutual funds. These UITs are sponsored by insurance companies, which are likely to be required to establish anti-money laundering programs in accordance with the BSA once a proposed rule is finalized.[62] Applying

---

[60] *See* Amendment to Bank Secrecy Act Regulations; Requirement that Brokers or Dealers in Securities Report Suspicious Transactions, 67 FR 44048 (July 1, 2002); 67 FR 21110, *supra* note 16. Treasury and the SEC have jointly proposed a rule that would require broker-dealers to establish and implement customer identification programs. *See* 67 FR 48306, *supra* note 17.

[61] Based on filings with the SEC, the SEC staff estimates that as of December 2001 there were approximately 683 unit investment trusts that were insurance company separate accounts, with aggregate assets of $650.5 billion.

[62] Insurance companies have long been defined as financial institutions for purposes of the BSA. *See* 15 U.S.C. 5312(a)(2)(M). In April 2002, Treasury temporarily deferred the anti-money laundering program requirement contained in section 352 of the USA Patriot Act that would have applied to insurance companies, to enable it to consider how anti-money laundering controls could best be applied to that industry, taking into account differences in size, location, and services within the industry. *See* 67 FR 21110, *supra* note 16. On September 26, 2002, Treasury

another set of anti-money laundering rules to such separate accounts appears unlikely to increase protection against money laundering.

B. Unregistered Investment Companies

In addition to "investment companies" that are required to be registered under the 1940 Act, there are similar pooled investment vehicles that are not "investment companies" for purposes of the 1940 Act that should be considered to be "investment companies" for purposes of the BSA. Such entities may include (i) privately offered funds that have a limited number of investors that rely on the exception in section 3(c)(1) of the 1940 Act; (ii) funds that are privately offered to qualified purchasers that rely on the exception in section 3(c)(7) of the 1940 Act; and (iii) entities that are not subject to the 1940 Act because they do not invest primarily in securities. These types of investment vehicles would include hedge funds, private equity funds, venture capital funds, commodity pools, and real estate investment trusts.[63]

1. Hedge Funds

The term "hedge fund" refers generally to a privately offered investment vehicle that pools the contributions of its investors in order to invest in a variety of asset classes, such as securities, futures contracts, options, bonds, and currencies.[64] A precise figure for the size of the

---

proposed a new rule that would prescribe minimum standards applicable to insurance companies pursuant to the BSA requirement that financial institutions establish anti-money laundering programs. *See* 67 FR 60625, *supra* note 16. The comment period on the proposed rule ends on November 25, 2002. *Id*

[63] As described in detail below, on September 26, 2002, FinCEN published a Notice of Proposed Rulemaking that would require many of these entities to establish anti-money laundering programs. 67 FR 60617, *supra* note 16, discussed at section III.B.4. of this report.

[64] The President's Working Group on Financial Markets describes a "hedge fund" as "any pooled investment vehicle that is privately organized, administered by professional investment managers, and not widely available to the public." Report of the President's Working Group on Financial Markets, "Hedge Funds, Leverage, and the Lessons of Long-Term Capital Management," at 1 (1999) ("Working Group Report"). It remains a matter of debate whether the term "hedge fund" refers only to funds that provide performance-based compensation for their managers, funds that actually hedge their exposure to the market, funds that engage in any investment strategy that is

hedge fund industry, in terms of the number of funds and the total value of assets managed, is unavailable because no official reporting organization exists for hedge funds. As of the last quarter of 2001, however, it was estimated that there were between 4,000 and 5,000 hedge funds worldwide that managed between $400 and $500 billion in capital.[65] Although the hedge fund industry remains small in relation to the mutual fund industry,[66] investment in hedge funds is growing.

Hedge funds domiciled in the United States are usually organized as limited partnerships or limited liability companies. The sponsor/general partner/manager usually holds an interest in the fund along with investors/limited partners/members,[67] who are, in most circumstances, either wealthy individuals or institutions such as savings associations, broker-dealers, investment companies, and employee benefit plans.[68] Further, hedge funds do not engage in "public offerings" of the interests in the funds. The sponsor often handles marketing and investor

---

intended to be non-correlated with the overall securities markets, funds that are not required to be registered, or some combination of the foregoing.

[65] *See* The Financial Stability Forum ("FSF") Recommendations and Concerns Raised by Highly Leveraged Institutions ("HLIs"): An Assessment, March 2002, at 1-2 (*http://www.fsforum.org/Reports/HLIreviewMar02.pdf*). The FSF is a 40-member organization convened in April 1999 by the Finance Ministers and Central Bank Governors of the G-7 countries.

[66] As discussed previously, as of December 2001, there were an estimated 8300 mutual funds with approximately $7 trillion in assets. *See* note 36 *infra* and accompanying text.

[67] The investors purchase interests in the hedge fund. These interests, whether denominated as units, shares or limited partnership interests, are securities. The Securities Act of 1933, however, provides an exemption from registration for securities that are not publicly offered. 15 U.S.C. 77d(2).

[68] Generally, hedge funds offer and sell interests to persons who qualify as "accredited investors," "qualified purchasers," or "qualified clients" as those terms are defined respectively for purposes of the Securities Act of 1933, the Investment Company Act of 1940, and the Investment Advisers Act of 1940. *See* 15 U.S.C. 77b(a)(15), 17 CFR 230.215, and 17 CFR 230.501 (defining "accredited investor"), 15 U.S.C. 80a-2(a)(51) (defining "qualified purchaser") and 17 CFR 275.205-3(d) (defining "qualified client"). Limiting investors in this way enables a fund to avoid registering the securities issued by the fund under the Securities Act of 1933, avoid registering the

services, and often serves as the fund manager with responsibility for making decisions regarding operations and investment strategy. A hedge fund also may retain an investment adviser or multiple advisers. It is not uncommon, however, for the sponsor, manager, and investment adviser(s) to be either the same legal entity or separate legal entities that might be owned by the sponsor. A typical hedge fund is similar to a mutual fund in that it maintains several contractual relationships that are integral to the operation of the hedge fund, including relationships with prime brokers, executing brokers, custodians, administrators, placement agents, registrars and transfer agents.[69]

For various reasons arising from tax, administrative, and regulatory concerns, hedge funds often are established under U.S. law as partnerships ("U.S. domestic hedge funds") or as corporations in a foreign jurisdiction ("U.S. hedge funds with an offshore related fund").[70] Hedge funds that are offered to U.S. investors tend to be structured in ways to address the needs of either tax-exempt investors or taxable investors. U.S. domestic hedge funds are usually in the form of limited partnerships to accommodate taxable U.S. investors. Partnerships provide favorable tax treatment for individual investors because the partnership's income is taxed only at the level of the individual investors in the partnership, as opposed to a corporation's income that is taxed at both the entity and individual investors' levels.[71] In contrast, some U.S. hedge funds

---

    fund itself under the Investment Company Act of 1940, and enables the fund to pay its investment adviser a performance-based fee, even if the adviser is registered with the SEC.

[69] Matthias Bekier, Marketing of Hedge Funds (1996), *excerpts available at* http://209.130.127.8/aimasite/research/bekierhf/hfstru23.htm.

[70] In addition, any of the persons contractually affiliated with a hedge fund (*e.g.*, prime broker, administrator, custodian, adviser, or distributor) may be located offshore.

[71] Some domestic hedge funds are organized as limited liability companies, which provide their investors with tax benefits identical to those of a limited partnership.

with an offshore related fund accommodate tax-exempt U.S. investors, such as pension funds and university endowments, and non-U.S. investors.[72]

Generally, all hedge funds require investors to complete subscription agreements that detail the investors' identity, domicile, and net worth, among other information.[73] The investor then returns the subscription agreement to the hedge fund manager or administrator and forwards his initial investment to the hedge fund's account with its custodian or its prime broker.[74] For the redemption of investment assets, U.S. domestic hedge funds usually rely on their custodian or prime broker to forward assets from the hedge fund's account to the investor's account. A U.S. hedge fund with an offshore related fund generally processes a redemption through its fund administrator, which sends the redeemed investment to the investor's bank account identified in the subscription documents.

A typical hedge fund often has a one-year "lock-up" period from the date of investment, during which the investor cannot redeem his investment.[75] Once the initial lock-up period is over, the right of an investor to redeem is governed by the partnership agreement. Most investors may demand a redemption during a set period that occurs on a quarterly, semi-annual,

---

[72] U.S. tax-exempt entities, such as university endowments and pension funds, are taxable on unrelated business taxable income ("UBIT") and therefore may seek to avoid the generation of income that the IRS may consider subject to UBIT by investing in an offshore fund that is a corporate entity.

[73] A subscription agreement is an agreement to buy shares or interests in a hedge fund. It also outlines the terms and conditions of redemptions and transfers of such shares or interests.

[74] Hedge funds rarely, if ever, receive or disburse currency to investors. Most investments are made by wire transfers from a financial institution, such as a bank, to the hedge fund's custodian or prime broker. When investors redeem their investments, most hedge funds forward the redemption proceeds to the account at the financial institution from which the initial investment was made.

[75] *See* Lori R. Runquist, *Hedge Funds: Alternative Investment Choices,* Market Signals Supplement, The Northern Trust Co., (Feb. 2002), at www.northernfunds.com/library/personal/mrkt_newsletters/money_matters/020200.pdf

or annual basis. There is no formal domestic secondary market for hedge fund shares.

Of the unregistered investment companies, hedge funds may be the most susceptible to abuse by money launderers because of the liquidity of their interests and their structure. Compared to the lock-up period imposed upon an investment by other unregistered investment companies, the lock-up period imposed upon an investment by a hedge fund is relatively short. Because money laundering has become such an expensive activity (estimated to cost 8%-10% of the amount of the money laundered), money launderers may be willing to invest their assets for a limited period to launder them in a manner that generates a return rather than a loss.

The structure of hedge funds also makes them vulnerable to money laundering. A U.S. *domestic* hedge fund is comprised of a general partner and a limited partner that form a U.S. limited partnership to hold a portfolio of liquid securities. A limited partner, either an individual or a corporate limited partner, could easily transfer the proceeds of crime into the hedge fund. Without anti-money laundering compliance responsibilities, a hedge fund has no responsibility to determine the source of an investor's funds or to analyze whether the source of those funds is questionable.

The U.S. hedge fund with an *offshore* related fund has a complex structure that begins with a general partner and limited partners in a U.S. limited partnership. The limited partnership often provides funds to an offshore corporate master, which invests the funds in a portfolio of liquid securities. The corporate master has an investment manager and an offshore administrator. The offshore corporate master also receives funds to invest from an offshore corporate feeder. The beneficial owners of the offshore corporate feeder may be composed of offshore investors and U.S. tax-exempt entities that invest offshore for tax purposes.

Depending on the jurisdiction in which the offshore corporate feeder is organized, it may be impossible to identify the beneficial owners of the money invested in the fund through the offshore corporate feeder or the source of the money being invested. The potential availability of "anonymous" investment and the inability of law enforcement to obtain information about the beneficial ownership of corporate entities in certain jurisdictions make this type of hedge fund particularly attractive to money launderers.[76] In fact, the Report of the President's Working Group on Financial Markets notes that a significant number of hedge funds have been established in offshore financial centers that are tax havens and may be engaged in or facilitating illegal tax avoidance and other inappropriate purposes.[77]

2. Commodity Pools

A commodity pool is an investment trust, syndicate or similar form of enterprise operated for trading commodity interests.[78] Commodity pool operators ("CPOs") are required to register with the CFTC as CPOs, and are subject to comprehensive regulation and oversight by the CFTC.[79] As of September 30, 2001, approximately 1,700 CPOs registered with the CFTC[80] operated an estimated 2,558 active commodity pools with $346 billion in assets.[81]

---

[76] *See Gilbert, supra* note 29.

[77] *See* Working Group Report, app. B at B-3.

[78] A "pool" is defined in 17 CFR 4.10(d), a rule promulgated by the CFTC under the Commodity Exchange Act ("CEA"), as "any investment trust, syndicate or similar form of enterprise operated for the purpose of trading commodity interests." As a general matter, there are two types of commodity pools: public pools and private pools. Securities issued by public pools (*i.e.,* pools offered through public offerings) are registered with the SEC under the Securities Act of 1933 and the Securities Exchange Act of 1934. If those public pools are investment companies, they also are registered with the SEC under the 1940 Act. Private pools (*i.e.,* pools that are offered through private placements) also may register with the SEC under the 1940 Act as investment companies.

[79] The CEA defines the term "commodity pool operator" as "any person engaged in a business that is of the nature of an investment trust, syndicate, or similar form of enterprise, and who, in connection therewith, solicits, accepts, or receives from others, funds, securities, or property, either directly or through capital contributions, the sale of stock or other forms of securities, or otherwise, for the purpose of trading in any commodity for future delivery on or subject to the rules of any contract market or derivatives transaction execution facility, except that the term

Pursuant to the CFTC's rules and depending upon the amount of assets in the pool, a CPO must provide investors and the CFTC with monthly or quarterly financial statements,[82] distribute and file an annual report for each pool that it operates,[83] and maintain and make available for CFTC inspection certain books and records.[84] CPOs also are subject to the general and specific anti-fraud provisions of the CEA and CFTC regulations.[85] The CFTC and the National Futures Association ("NFA"), the futures industry's self-regulatory organization, review all of the commodity pools' annual financial statements. Further, each CPO must complete an annual self-audit questionnaire and undergo an onsite examination by NFA approximately once every 2.5 years. That examination covers the CPO itself and every commodity pool operated by the CPO. NFA maintains a publicly available database that can be used by both regulators and investors and contains the names, addresses, NFA identification numbers, regulatory history, and other pertinent information regarding the CPOs and commodity pools.[86]

---

does not include such persons not within the intent of the definition of the term as the Commission may specify by rule, regulation, or order." 7 U.S.C. 1a(5).

[80] CFTC 2001 Annual Report, "Futures Industry Registrants by Location as of September 30, 2001," at 150.

[81] This information is based on estimates supplied to the staff of the CFTC by the National Futures Association.

[82] 17 CFR 4.22.

[83] 17 CFR 4.22(c). Before a commodity pool can accept funds or other property from investors in the pool, the CPO must distribute and file a disclosure document with the CFTC and National Futures Association. 17 CFR 4.21, 4.24-4.26.

[84] 17 CFR 4.23.

[85] 7 U.S.C. 6b prohibits fraudulent activity in or in connection with a futures contract. 7 U.S.C. 6o prohibits fraudulent transactions by CPOs and CTAs. 17 CFR 32.9 and 33.10 bar fraud by any person in connection with commodity option transactions.

[86] The National Futures Association database can be searched on the Internet at http://www.nfa.futures.org/basic. As described in detail below, on September 26, 2002, FinCEN

3. Private Equity and Venture Capital Funds

Private equity funds are vehicles in which investors pool money to invest in unregistered securities of public or private companies that have been in existence for several years and have established products, customers, and operating records. A venture capital fund is a type of private equity fund[87] in which participants pool capital to invest in the seed, start-up or early stages of companies. These funds[88] do not engage in public offerings and generally have a small number of institutional and wealthy individual investors.[89]

There is little information on the number of private equity funds and the total value of assets managed by such funds because, like hedge funds, there is no official reporting organization that exists for private equity funds. However, in 2001, an estimated 1,627 venture capital funds were in existence with $250 billion in capital under management.[90]

Private equity funds are sponsored by private equity firms, which typically sponsor more than one fund. Each fund, however, is organized as a separate legal entity. Most private equity funds are structured as limited partnerships with the general partner being the private equity firm

---

published a notice or proposed rulemaking that would require commodity pools, and therefore, CPOs indirectly, to establish anti-money laundering programs. 67 FR 60617, *supra* note 16, discussed at section III.B.4. of this report.

[87] There are other types of private equity funds including leveraged buyout funds, which finance the purchase of established companies; mezzanine funds, which are used to purchase and recapitalize private companies; and opportunity funds, which invest in distressed companies. However, most of the details and descriptions in this report focus on the practices of private equity funds generally and venture capital funds which are a subset of private equity funds.

[88] For purposes of this report, both types of funds will be referred to generally as "private equity funds."

[89] *See supra* note 77 regarding "accredited investors," "qualified purchasers," and "qualified clients."

[90] The NVCA 2002 Yearbook, National Venture Capital Association ("NVCA"), ("The NVCA 2002 Yearbook"), at *http://www.nvca.org*.

and the investors serving as limited partners.[91] Typically, the general partner serves as the fund's manager and is responsible for researching the companies in which the fund might invest.[92] In some instances, particularly in venture capital funds, the general partner plays an active role in the companies in which the fund invests, either by sitting on the board of directors or becoming involved in day-to-day management. The general partner establishes a management company to handle routine administrative matters such as administering payroll and benefits for the fund's employees, leasing office space, and recording the limited partners' investments in the fund.

Many private equity funds establish offshore mirror funds. These offshore funds have separate limited partners from the domestic fund, but the funds invest in the same or similar companies. Funds with an offshore element can be structured in a number of ways, but the general partner of the companion U.S. fund generally manages them.[93] As with hedge funds, the investors in offshore private equity funds are typically U.S. tax-exempt organizations and foreign persons or institutions.

The general partner of a private equity fund "solicits" investors directly—there is no general advertisement or public offering of the fund's securities.[94] Investors typically include

---

[91] Some private equity funds are organized as limited liability companies and, occasionally, corporations.

[92] Depending on the size of the fund and the types of investors, the manager may be required to register as an investment adviser under the 1940 Act, 15 U.S.C. 80b-1 *et seq.* But, generally, private equity funds are subject to limited government regulation.

[93] Regardless of the structure of the onshore/offshore arrangement, the general partner's management company in the U.S. typically has custody of the records of all of the investors, although there is often a copy of the records for the offshore investors kept in the jurisdiction of the offshore fund. In the case of a fund that has some U.S. investors but is strictly an offshore fund (*i.e.*, organized by non-U.S. general partners), such records typically will be kept offshore.

[94] Private equity funds are not required to provide disclosure information to investors. Nonetheless, they typically provide offering memoranda to prospective investors. The general partners of private equity funds usually collect a large amount of information about prospective limited

high net worth individuals and families, pension funds, endowment organizations, banks and insurance companies.[95]

In most cases, private equity funds have a lifespan of 10 to 12 years, although the investment in each portfolio company usually lasts for a shorter period, such as 3 to 7 years.[96] Investors commit to invest a certain amount of money with the fund over the life of the fund. Investors make their contributions to the fund in response to "capital calls" from the general partner. Capital calls are made when the general partner has identified a portfolio company in which the private equity fund will invest and needs access to capital to make the investment. Once an investor meets the capital call, the private equity fund invests the new capital in the portfolio company almost immediately. The private equity fund typically does not retain a pool of uninvested capital.[97]

Private equity funds are long-term investments and provide little, if any, opportunity for investors to redeem their investments.[98] There is no formal secondary market for shares in a

---

partners to confirm that the limited partners will be able to meet their capital commitments when required by the private equity fund.

[95] Industry sources estimate that individuals and families account for less than 10% of the assets invested in private equity funds, pension funds account for about 30%, endowments account for about 20%, and banks and insurance companies account for about 40%. The NVCA estimates that individuals and families account for approximately 10% of the invested assets in venture capital funds, pension funds account for 40%, endowments account for 20%; and banks, insurance companies and corporations account for about 30%. The NVCA 2002 Yearbook, *supra* note 90

[96] The term of existence of each private equity fund is found in the fund's partnership agreement.

[97] Investors' contributions are wired to the private equity fund's bank account from which they are routed to the portfolio company. The administrative arm of the private equity fund is responsible for keeping records of investors' contributions and distributions.

[98] Although a private equity fund rarely redeems its investors' shares in the fund, the fund may pay its investors dividends. A private equity fund may distribute a cash dividend to its investors when it profits from the sale of a particular portfolio investment or may distribute a stock dividend to its investors when it receives shares in a particular portfolio company after the company has

private equity fund, although there is a small informal secondary market that is comprised of private equity funds specializing in buying interests in established funds.[99]

4. Real Estate Investment Trusts ("REITs")

A REIT is an investment vehicle that allows investors to own interests in income-producing real estate properties or participate in mortgage financing.[100] There are three basic types of REITs: equity REITS, mortgage REITs and hybrid REITS. Equity REITs, which own and operate income-producing real estate, account for 96.1% of REITS. Mortgage REITs, which lend money directly to real estate owners and operators or extend credit indirectly through the acquisition of loan interests, account for 1.6% of REITS. Hybrid REITs, which both own properties and make loans to real estate owners and operators, account for 2.3% of REITS.[101]

The structure of a typical REIT is dictated by certain provisions of the Internal Revenue Code ("IRC").[102] A REIT must be organized as a corporation, trust or association that would be subject to U.S. corporate income taxation but for the REIT provisions of the IRC.[103] The IRC also requires that a REIT be managed by a board of directors or trustees, have shares that are fully transferable, have a minimum of 100 shareholders, have no more than 50% of its shares

---

undergone an initial public offering. To facilitate the transfer of shares from the fund to its investors in the case of a stock dividend, the fund usually retains the services of a transfer agent.

[99] In 1999, five private equity funds raised $1.6 billion for purchases of secondary interests in other private equity funds. *See* David M. Toll, "Private Equity Primer," in *Galante's Venture Capital & Private Equity Directory*.

[100] A REIT is not an investment company under the 1940 Act. *See* 15 U.S.C. 80a-3(a)(1)(A) (defining investment companies to be in the business of investing, reinvesting, or trading in securities) and 15 U.S.C. 80a-3(c)(5)(C) (excluding from the definition of investment companies certain issuers that are engaged primarily in the business of purchasing or otherwise acquiring mortgages or other liens on an interests in real estate.)

[101] These statistics are available from the National Association of Real Estate Investment Trusts ("NAREIT"), at *www.nareit.com*.

[102] Subchapter M of the Internal Revenue Code, 26 U.S.C. 851 *et seq.*

[103] 26 U.S.C. 856.

held by five or fewer individuals during the last half of each taxable year, invest at least 75% of its total assets in real estate assets, derive at least 75% of its gross income from rents from real property or interest on mortgages on real property, have no more than 20% of its assets consist of stocks in taxable REIT subsidiaries, and pay at least 90% of its taxable income to investors in the form of dividends.[104]

According to industry sources, as of March 2001 there were approximately 300 REITs operating in the U.S. with assets totaling over $300 billion.[105] Currently, approximately 190 large REITs are registered with the SEC as public companies under the Securities Exchange Act of 1934 and trade on the national stock exchanges.[106] The securities of REITs registered with the SEC are traded through broker-dealers, which are already subject to anti-money laundering regulations promulgated under the BSA. Approximately 100 private REITs, entities whose securities are not listed on a securities exchange, are in existence. The typical life span of a private REIT is 10 to 15 years. They are similar to the publicly listed and traded REITS in terms of structure due to the requirements of the IRC. The securities of the private REIT may be registered with the SEC under the Securities Act of 1933 or may be private placements. In most cases, investors purchase private REIT securities through an SEC-registered broker-dealer. Most private REITs provide investors with the opportunity to purchase additional shares through a dividend reinvestment program. An investment in a private REIT tends to be illiquid because the

---

[104] *Id.*

[105] *See* www.investinreits.com/faqtext.cfm#how_many

[106] According to NAREIT, there are approximately 149 REITs listed on the New York Stock Exchange, 27 REITs listed on the American Stock Exchange, and 12 REITs listed on the NASDAQ National Market System. *See* "Frequently Asked Questions about REITs," *at* http://www.nareit.com/aboutreits/faqtext.cfm

investors usually have no right to redeem their interests and the REIT often restricts the transfer of interests to comply with other IRC requirements.

5. Proposed Rule for the Application of the BSA to Unregistered Investment Companies

The rule that temporarily exempts investment companies other than mutual funds from the BSA requirement that investment companies implement anti-money laundering programs, applies to all unregistered investment companies.[107] However, in that rule, FinCEN observed that a number of unregistered entities such as hedge funds are excluded from the 1940 Act definition of "investment company" and that those entities would likely be required to establish anti-money laundering programs under section 352 of the USA Patriot Act in the future.[108]

With respect to investment companies not registered under the 1940 Act, Treasury considered two different approaches in creating an appropriate definition. Treasury could have defined, to the extent possible, the various sub-categories of unregistered investment companies (such as hedge funds, private equity funds, and venture capital funds) and then could have fashioned regulations for each sub-category based on the extent to which that sub-category is vulnerable to money laundering. One disadvantage of such an approach is that the labels for many of these entities are somewhat colloquial in nature and are not susceptible to precise definition. Thus, this approach risked failing to capture companies that have characteristics that would enable them to be used for money laundering. At the other extreme, including every perceivable sub-category of entities would unnecessarily burden businesses that money launderers are unlikely to use. Moreover, an overly inclusive definition would bring within the scope of the BSA's anti-money laundering requirements so many entities as to tax resources of

---

[107] 67 FR 21117, *supra* note 16.
[108] *Id.* at n.5.

the federal regulatory agencies charged with oversight of financial institutions and, thus, diminish the effectiveness of that oversight.

Treasury proposed an alternative approach in defining unregistered investment companies: consider the group as a whole and define the characteristics of such entities that present money laundering risks. This approach subjects entities to regulation under the BSA only if they possess those characteristics that present cognizable risks of money laundering.

On September 26, 2002, FinCEN issued a proposed rule that would require certain "unregistered investment companies," including certain entities that rely on the exceptions in sections 3(c)(1) and 3(c)(7) of the Investment Company Act, commodity pools, and REITs, to develop and implement anti-money laundering programs reasonably designed to prevent them from being used to launder money or finance terrorist activities.[109] The proposed rule was carefully designed to balance the need for a comprehensive national program to prevent money laundering against the burdens imposed by the BSA on businesses, including small businesses.

Under the proposed rule, an "unregistered investment company" is an issuer of securities that (i) would be an investment company under the 1940 Act, but for the exclusions provided in sections 3(c)(1) and 3(c)(7) of that Act; (ii) is a commodity pool; or (iii) invests primarily in real estate and/or interests therein.[110] Because of the broad scope of the type and nature of businesses that fall within these categories, FinCEN proposed to further narrow the definition of

---

[109] *See* 67 FR 60617, 60618, *supra* note 16.

[110] This definition thus would include entities consisting of pools of three asset classes: securities, commodity futures contracts, and real estate. The notice of proposed rulemaking requests comment whether there are other entities, not covered by other rules requiring anti-money laundering programs, that pool assets and provide a similar opportunity for money laundering or terrorist financing, and whether such entities should be required by the final rule to establish anti-money laundering programs.

unregistered investment company by several limitations and exceptions from the definition, as described below.

Redemption Rights. FinCEN proposed to define "unregistered investment company" to include only those companies that permit an investor to redeem a portion of his or her investment within two years after that investment was made. Investment companies rarely receive from or disburse to investors significant amounts of currency. Therefore, if these companies are used to launder money, they are more likely to be used as a transition method of investment, in order to obscure the source and eventual use of tainted proceeds. The use of financial institutions at this stage of the process generally requires that the money launderer be able to redeem his or her interests in the company within a relatively short period. Conversely, companies whose shares are not redeemable, or whose shares are redeemable only after a lengthy holding (or "lock-up") period, generally lack the liquidity that makes them attractive to money launderers. The proposed rule's "redeemability" requirement will likely have the effect of excluding from the rule publicly traded REITs, a large number of special purpose financing vehicles, and many private equity and venture capital funds.

Minimum Asset Size. Some entities, such as small businesses and investment clubs, are so small that they are unlikely to be used for money laundering.[111] Therefore, the Proposed Rule would exclude from its coverage companies with less than $1,000,000 in assets as of the end of the most recent calendar quarter.

Offshore Funds. Because many unregistered investment companies operate "offshore" and offer interests to both U.S. and foreign persons, the rule would extend to funds that (i) are

---

[111] FinCEN believes that entities with less than $1,000,000 in assets pose significantly lower money laundering risks than larger entities. *See also* section 312(a)(4)(b) of the USA Patriot Act (defining "private banking account" to include accounts of not less than $1,000,000).

organized in the United States; (ii) are organized or sponsored by a U.S. person; or (iii) sell ownership interests to U.S. persons.[112] Treasury proposed the rule having a long jurisdictional reach to prevent circumvention of the rule by money launderers who could easily shift operations to a hedge fund organized offshore in a jurisdiction that did not have adequate laws prohibiting money laundering. The proposed rule reflects Treasury's determination that it is appropriate and reasonable to require issuers that benefit from the financial and legal systems of the United States to establish anti-money laundering programs to prevent, detect, and facilitate the prosecution of international money laundering and terrorist financing.

Exceptions. FinCEN proposed to except from the rule investment companies that are (i) family companies, (ii) employee securities companies, and (iii) employee benefit plans that are not construed to be pools in CFTC Rule 4.5(a)(4).[113] These types of companies are unlikely to be used for money laundering purposes by third parties given their size, structure and purpose. The proposed rule also excepts other types of financial institutions under the BSA to prevent duplicative application of the BSA anti-money laundering rules to the same financial institution.

Notice. The proposed rule would require a company falling within the definition to file a brief notice with FinCEN containing basic information about the company, such as its legal name and address, the name and contact information of its anti-money laundering program compliance officer, the dollar amount of the assets under its management, and the number of investors in the company. The notice will enable Treasury or its designee to identify unregistered investment companies subject to the rule and to monitor their compliance.

---

[112] The rule would not apply, however, to an unregistered fund that is merely advised by a U.S. person because such a person would be unlikely to be in a position to administer the rule.

[113] 17 CFR 4.5. CFTC Rule 4.5(a)(4) sets forth the employee benefit plans that are not construed to be pools.

IV. Personal Holding Companies

Section 356 also requires that the report include recommendations on whether the Secretary should promulgate regulations requiring "personal holding companies" to disclose their beneficial owners when opening accounts or initiating transfers at any domestic financial institution.

The USA Patriot Act defines a personal holding company as a business, including a corporation or business or other grantor trust whose assets are predominantly securities, bank certificates of deposit, or other securities or investment instruments (other than those relating to operating subsidiaries of the corporation or trust) and that has 5 or fewer common shareholders or holders of beneficial or other equity interest.[114]

Personal holding companies may be located anywhere in the world and can be defined in several ways. In the United States, the Internal Revenue Code defines a personal holding company[115] and a foreign personal holding company[116] by reference to the amount of passive income it earns and whether it is closely held. Moreover, certain foreign jurisdictions offer asset management vehicles that they describe as personal holding companies, which are often intended for use by high net worth individuals as a means of managing wealth.

Personal holding companies, which are also known as personal investment companies, may be used by individuals as vehicles for managing their personal finances, estate planning, and

---

[114] In the event that a personal holding company beneficially owned by a non-U.S. person establishes or maintains a "private banking account" (as defined in section 312 of the USA PATRIOT Act) with a U.S. financial institution, the institution would be required by Section 312 to identify, and perform other due diligence with respect to, such beneficial owner and account.

[115] 26 U.S.C. 542

[116] 26 U.S.C. 552

other purposes. In addition, entrepreneurs may use personal holding companies to better diversify their investment risk, or manage their personal finances.

The issue of whether and to what extent additional anti-money laundering controls may be needed for a variety of different types of asset management vehicles and products is one that Treasury continues to study, drawing on the knowledge and expertise of others within the Federal regulatory community and within law enforcement. It is important to ensure that a balance is struck between the potential for abuse of asset management vehicles, such as trusts, personal holding companies, and other vehicles, and the limitation and costs resulting from regulatory requirements. Regulatory requirements may have the unintended economic effect of limiting access to such asset management vehicles. At this time, no additional recommendations regarding anti-money laundering controls for personal holding companies are being made.

V. Recommendations

Treasury and the federal functional regulators have greatly expanded the scope and reach of regulations under the BSA since Congress passed the USA Patriot Act approximately one year ago. This report has described regulations, some final, some proposed, that have been promulgated to deter criminals and terrorists from laundering money through the various entities defined as financial institutions under the BSA. Some of these regulations apply to various types of investment companies, both registered and unregistered. This section of the report will briefly summarize the regulations promulgated to date, the regulations that are still under consideration, and the recommendations for regulatory action by the Treasury, the SEC and the Federal Reserve Board.

REGISTERED INVESTMENT COMPANIES:

Mutual Funds:

- Interim Final Regulation requiring the establishment of an anti-money laundering program (issued April 26, 2002). [67 FR 21117]
- Proposed Regulation requiring establishment of customer identification programs (issued July 23, 2002). [67 FR 48318]
- Proposed Regulation requiring implementation of due diligence programs for correspondent and private banking accounts (issued May 30, 2002). [67 FR 37736]
- Final Regulation setting forth procedures for information sharing between federal law enforcement agencies and financial institutions and permitting voluntary information sharing among financial institutions (issued September 26, 2002) [67 FR 48348]
- Treasury recommends requiring mutual funds to file suspicious activity reports.

Closed-End Funds:

- No regulations are recommended for these investment companies. Because these funds' securities operate much like securities issued by a corporation, these funds do not appear to present a money laundering risk sufficient to warrant regulation at this time.
- In an interval fund (a type of closed-end fund with limited repurchase rights), investors do not control either the timing or the amount of a repurchase offer. As a result, it does not appear that these funds present a money laundering risk sufficient to warrant regulation at this time.

Unit Investment Trusts (UITs):

- These funds' securities are available only through broker-dealers or life insurance companies. Registered broker-dealers are subject to both anti-money laundering and (as of January 1, 2003) SAR reporting regulations (issued April 29, 2002 and July 1, 2002). [67 FR 21110; 67 FR 44048] Treasury and the SEC have jointly proposed to require registered broker-dealers to adopt and implement customer identification programs (issued July 23, 2002). [67 FR 48306] Treasury has proposed regulations requiring life insurance companies to implement anti-money laundering compliance programs and to file SARs (issued September 26, 2002 and October 17, 2002) [67 FR 60625; 67 FR 64067]. No new regulations are recommended for these investment companies.

UNREGISTERED INVESTMENT COMPANIES:

- Proposed regulation requiring certain unregistered investment companies to establish anti-money laundering programs (issued September 26, 2002). [67 FR 60617]
- Treasury recommends requiring unregistered investment companies to establish customer identification and verification programs.

PERSONAL HOLDING COMPANIES

- No regulations are recommended for personal holding companies.